AF496758

[259] DEDICATION

To TIMOTHY BROWN, Esq.

OF PECKHAM LODGE, SURREY

North Hempstead, Long Island,
10th Dec. 1818.

MY DEAR SIR,

THE little volume here presented to the public, consists, as you will perceive, for the greater and most valuable part, of travelling notes made by our friend HULME, whom I had the honour to introduce to you in 1816, and with whom you were so much pleased.

His activity, which nothing can benumb; his zeal against the twin monster, tyranny and priestcraft, which nothing can cool; and his desire to assist in providing a place of retreat for the oppressed, which nothing but the success in the accomplishment can satisfy; these have induced him to employ almost the whole of his time here in various ways all tending to the same point.

The Boroughmongers have agents and spies all over the inhabited globe. Here they cannot *sell blood*: they can only collect information and calumniate the people of both countries. These vermin our friend *firks out* (as the Hampshire people call it); and they hate him as rats hate a terrier.

Amongst his other labours, he has performed a very laborious journey to the *Western Countries*, and has been as far as the Colony [260] of our friend BIRKBECK. This journey has produced a JOURNAL; and this Journal, along with the rest of the volume, I dedicate to you in testimony of my constant remembrance of the many, many happy hours I have spent with you, and of the numerous acts of kindness which I have received at your hands.   You were one of those, who *sought acquaintance with me*, when I was shut up in a felon's jail *for two years* for having expressed my indignation at seeing Englishmen flogged, in the heart of England, under a guard of German bayonets and sabres, and when I had on my head *a thousand pounds fine* and *seven years' recognizances*.   You, at the end of the two years, took me from the prison, in your carriage, home to your house.   You and our kind friend, WALKER, are *even yet*, held in bonds for my *good behaviour*, the seven years not being expired. All these things are written in the very core of my heart; and when I act as if I had forgotten any one of them, may no name on earth be so much detested and despised as that of

Your faithful friend,
And most obedient servant,
WM. COBBETT

[261] PREFACE

In giving an account of the United States of America, it would not have been proper to omit saying something of the *Western Countries*, the Newest of the New Worlds, to which so many thousands and hundreds of thousands are flocking, and towards which the writings of Mr. Birkbeck have, of late, drawn the pointed attention of all those Englishmen, who, having something left to be robbed of, and wishing to preserve it, are looking towards America as a place of refuge from the Boroughmongers and the Holy Alliance, which latter, to make the compact complete, seems to want nothing but the accession of His Satanic Majesty.

I *could not go* to the Western Countries; and the accounts of others were seldom to be relied on; because, scarcely any man goes thither without some degree of partiality, or comes back without being tainted with some little matter, at least, of self-interest. Yet, it was desirable to make an attempt, at least, towards settling the question: "Whether the Atlantic, or the Western, Countries were the best for *English Farmers* to settle in." Therefore, when Mr. Hulme proposed to make a Western Tour, I was very [262] much pleased, seeing that, of all the men I knew, he was the most likely to bring us back an *impartial* account of what he should see. His great knowledge of farming as well as of manufacturing affairs; his capacity of estimating local advantages and disadvantages; the natural turn of his mind for discovering the means of applying to the use of man all that is furnished by the testimony of my constant remembrance of the many, many happy hours I have spent with you, and of the numerous acts of kindness which I have received at your hands. You were one of those, who *sought acquaintance with me*, when I was shut up in a felon's jail *for two years* for having expressed my indignation at seeing Englishmen flogged, in the heart of England, under a guard of German bayonets and sabres, and when I had on my head *a thousand pounds fine* and *seven years' recognizances* You, at the end of the two years, took me from the prison, in your carriage, home to your house. You and our kind friend, WALKER, are *even yet*, held in bonds for my *good behaviour*, the seven years not being expired. All these things are written in the very core of my heart; and when I act as if I had forgotten any one of them, may no name on earth be so much detested and despised as that of

> Your faithful friend,
> And most obedient servant,
> WM. COBBETT

In giving an account of the United States of America, it would not have been proper to omit saying something of the *Western Countries*, the Newest of the New Worlds, to which so many thousands and hundreds of thousands are flocking, and towards which the writings of Mr. Birkbeck have, of late, drawn the pointed attention of all those Englishmen, who, having something left to be robbed of, and wishing to preserve it, are looking towards America as a place of refuge from the Boroughmongers and the Holy Alliance, which latter, to make the compact complete, seems to want nothing but the accession of His Satanic Majesty.

I *could not go* to the Western Countries; and the accounts of others were seldom to be relied on; because, scarcely any man goes thither without some degree of partiality, or comes back without being tainted with some little matter, at least, of self-interest. Yet, it was desirable to make an attempt, at least, towards settling the question: "Whether the Atlantic, or the Western, Countries were the best for *English Farmers* to settle in." Therefore, when Mr. HULME proposed to make a Western Tour, I was very [262] much pleased, seeing that, of all the men I knew, he was the most likely to bring us back an *impartial* account of what he should see. His great knowledge of farming as well as of manufacturing affairs; his capacity of estimating local advantages and disadvantages; the natural turn of his mind for discovering the means of applying to the use of man all that is furnished by the earth, the air, and water; the patience and perseverance with which he pursues all his inquiries; the urbanity of his manners, which opens to him all the sources of information; his inflexible adherence to *truth*. all these marked him out as the man on whom the public might safely rely.

I, therefore, give his Journal, made during his tour. He offers no *opinion* as to the *question* above stated. That *I shall* do; and when the reader has gone through the Journal he will find my opinions as to that question, which opinions I have stated in a Letter addressed to Mr. BIRKBECK.

The American reader will perceive, that this Letter is intended principally for the perusal of *Englishmen*; and, therefore, he must not be surprised if he finds a little bickering in a group so much of a *family* cast.

WM. COBBETT

North Hempstead,
10th December, 1818.

[263] INTRODUCTION TO THE JOURNAL

Philadelphia, 30th Sept. 1818.

IT seems necessary, by way of Introduction to the following *Journal*, to say some little matter respecting the author of it, and also respecting his motives for wishing it to be published.

As to the first, I am an Englishman by birth and parentage; and am of the county of Lancaster. I was bred and brought up at farming work, and became an apprentice to the business of *Bleacher*, at the age of 14 years. My own industry made me a master-bleacher, in which state I lived many years at Great Lever, near Bolton, where I employed about 140 men, women, and children, and had generally about 40 apprentices. By this business, pursued with incessant application, I had acquired, several years ago, property to an amount sufficient to satisfy any man of moderate desires.

But, along with my money my children had come and had gone on increasing to the number of *nine*. New *duties* now arose, and demanded my best attention. It was not sufficient that I was likely to have a decent fortune for each child. I was bound to provide, if possible, against my children being stripped of what I had earned for them. I, therefore, looked seriously at the situation of England; and, I saw, that the incomes of my children were all *pawned* (as my friend Cobbett[1] truly calls it) to

---

[1] For a brief biography of William Cobbett, see Flint's *Letters*, volume ix of our series, note 4.— ED.

pay the Debts of the Borough, or seat, owners. I saw
that, of whatever I might be able to [264] give to my children, as well as of what they might be able to earn, *more
than one half* would be taken away to feed pensioned
Lords and Ladies, Soldiers to shoot at us, Parsons to
persecute us, and Fundholders, who had lent their money
to be applied to purposes of enslaving us. This view of
the matter was sufficient to induce the father of nine children to think of the means of rescuing them from the
consequences, which common sense taught him to appre-
hend. But, there were other considerations, which oper-
ated with me in producing my emigration to America.

In the year 1811 and 1812 the part of the country, in
which I lived, was placed under a *new sort of law*; or, in
other words, it was placed out of the protection of the old
law of the land.[2] Men were seized, dragged to prison,
treated like convicts, many transported and put to death,
without having committed any thing, which the law of
the land deems a *crime*. It was then that the infamous
Spy-System was again set to work in Lancashire, in which
horrid system FLETCHER of Bolton was one of the prin-

[2] In 1811 the growing hostility of those employed in the manufacture of
stockings to the introduction of knitting frames, culminated in the Luddite
Riots, and in Nottingham over six hundred stocking frames were broken. The
riot spread rapidly among the artisans in the cotton and woolen industries in
Lancashire and Yorkshire, mills were burned, machinery of all kinds destroyed,
and it became necessary to call out seven regiments before quiet was restored.
The government became alarmed, especially as the mobs had stormed the
militia depots and secured arms for themselves, and several repressive measures
were hurried through Parliament. The first, passed March 5, 1812, made frame-
breaking a capital offense; the second, the Nottingham Watch and Ward Bill,
passed the same month, enabled the lord-lieutenant or sheriff to establish
watch and ward if further riots occurred; and the third, the Preservation of
Public Peace Act, passed July 27, 1812, empowered any magistrate in the dis-
turbed district to search for secreted arms, and to call upon the people to give up
their weapons. See *Parliamentary Debates*, xxi, pp. 859, 1166; xxiii, pp. 1099,
1251.— ED.

cipal actors, or, rather, organizers and promoters. At this time I endeavoured to detect the machinations of these dealers in human blood; and, I narrowly escaped being sacrificed myself on the testimony of two men, who had their pardon offered them on condition of their *swearing against me*. The men refused, and were transported, leaving wives and children to starve.

Upon this occasion, my friend DOCTOR TAYLOR, most humanely, and with his usual zeal and talent, laboured to counteract the works of FLETCHER and his associates. The DOCTOR published a pamphlet on the subject, in 1812, which every Englishman should read. I, as far as I was able, co-operated with him. We went to London, laid the real facts before several members of the two houses of Parliament; and, in some degree, checked the progress of the dealers in blood. I had an interview with Lord Holland, and told him, that, if he would pledge himself to cause the *secret-service money* to be kept in London, I would pledge myself for the keeping of the peace in Lancashire. In [265] short, it was necessary, in order to support the tyranny of the seat-sellers, that *terror* should prevail in the populous districts. *Blood* was wanted to flow; and *money* was given to spies to tempt men into what the new law had made crimes.

From this time I resolved *not to leave my children in such a state of things*, unless I should be taken off very suddenly. I saw no hope of obtaining *a Reform of the Parliament*, without which it was clear to me, that the people of England must continue to work solely for the benefit of the great insolent families, whom I hated for their injustice and rapacity, and despised for their meanness and ignorance. I saw, in them, a mass of debauched and worthless beings, having at their command an army to compel the people to surrender to them the fruits of their industry; and in addition, a body existing under the garb of *religion*, almost as despicable in point of character, and still more malignant.

I could not have died in peace, leaving my children the slaves of such a set of beings; and I could not live in peace, knowing, that at any hour, I might die and so leave my family. Therefore I resolved, like the Lark in the fable, to *remove* my brood, which was still more numerous than that of the Lark. While the war was going on between England and America, I could not come to this country. Besides, I had great affairs to arrange. In 1816, having made my preparations, I set off, *not with my family*; for that I did not think a prudent step. It was necessary for me to *see* what America really was. I therefore, came for that purpose.

I was well pleased with America, over a considerable part of which I travelled. I saw an absence of human misery. I saw a government taking away a very small portion of men's earnings. I saw ease and happiness and a fearless utterance of thought every where prevail. I saw laws like those of the *old laws* of England, every where obeyed with cheerfulness and held in veneration. I heard of no mobs, no riots, no spies, no transportings, no hangings. I saw those very *Irish*, to keep whom in order, such murderous laws exist in [266] Ireland, here good, peaceable, industrious citizens. I saw no placemen and pensioners, riding the people under foot. I saw no greedy Priesthood, fattening on the fruits of labour in which they had never participated, and which fruits they seized in despite of the people. I saw a *Debt*, indeed, but then, it was so insignificant a thing; and, besides, it had been contracted for *the people's use*, and not for that of a set of tyrants, who had used the money to *the injury of the peo-*

ple. In short, I saw a state of things, precisely the reverse of that in England, and very nearly what it would be in England, if the Parliament were reformed.

Therefore, in the Autumn of 1816, I returned to England fully intending to return the next spring with my family and whatever I possessed of the fruits of my labours, and to make America my country and the country of that family. Upon my return to England, however, I found a great stir about *Reform*;[3] and having, in their full force, all those feelings, which make our native country dear to us, I said, at once, "My desire is, not to change country or countrymen, but to change slavery for freedom: give me freedom here, and here I'll remain." These are nearly the very words that I uttered to Mr. COBBETT, when first introduced to him, in December 1816, by that excellent man, MAJOR CARTWRIGHT.[4] Nor was I unwilling to *labour myself* in the cause of Reform. I was one of

---

[3] The year 1816 was a time of intense suffering among the working classes in England. Corn reached famine prices, and at the same time the return of peace, by reducing the foreign demand for manufactured articles, created an over supply of labor Riots again occurred, but the general discontent found a new outlet in the demand for parliamentary reform. In this, Cobbett was the leader, and under his direction Hampden Clubs were established all over the country Sir Francis Burdett, president of the London Hampden Club, was first chosen to further the cause in the House of Commons. A graduate of Oxford, he entered Parliament in 1796, when twenty-six years of age, and served almost continuously until his death, in 1844. He was throughout an earnest advocate of parliamentary reform, of freedom of speech in the House, and of other liberal measures. Cobbett, Hulme, and the Radicals disliked him because his methods were too moderate for them. The incident mentioned by Hulme refers to a large meeting held at London at the end of the year (1816), to which all the Hampden Clubs sent delegates; and to avoid which Sir Francis, who had a horror of popular demonstrations, fled to Leicestershire, and sent a letter stating his inability to be present See Cobbett, *Weekly Political Register*, September 13, 1817.— ED

[4] Next to Cobbett, the most important leader of the reform movement during this period was Major John Cartwright. Born in Nottinghamshire (1740), he had entered the navy and was being promoted rapidly when he refused to join his commander, Lord Howe, against the American colonies, thus putting an end to his professional advancement Turning his attention to politics, he

those very *Delegates*, of whom the Borough-tyrants said so many falsehoods, and whom SIR FRANCIS BURDETT so shamefully abandoned.   In the meeting of Delegates, I thought we went too far in reposing confidence in him: I spoke my opinion as to this point: and, in a very few days, I had the full proof of the correctness of my opinion.   I was present when MAJOR CARTWRIGHT opened a letter from SIR FRANCIS, which had come from *Leicestershire*. I thought the kind-hearted old Major would have dropped upon the floor!   I shall never forget his looks as he read that letter.   If the paultry Burdett had a hundred lives, the taking of them all away would not atone for the pain he that day gave to Major Cartwright, not to mention the pain [267] given to others, and the injury done to the cause.   For my part, I was not much disappointed. I had no opinion of Sir Francis Burdett's being sound. He seemed to me too much attached to his *own importance* to do the people any real service.   He is an *aristocrat*; and that is enough for me.   It is folly to suppose, that such a man will *ever* be a real friend of the rights of the people. I wish he were *here* a little while.   He would soon find his proper level; and that would not, I think, be very high.   Mr. HUNT[5] was very much against our confiding

began (1780) the agitation which earned for him the title of Father of Reform. He was a frequent contributor to Cobbett's *Register*, in the cause of parliamentary and other reforms — ED.

[5] Henry Hunt, familiarly known as Orator Hunt (1773-1835), belonged to a Wiltshire family.   He was engaged in farming near Bristol when, during a visit to London (1807), he became interested in the Radical cause, and immediately set to work to organize the Radical party in Bristol and the surrounding country.   An eloquent speaker, and of magnetic personality, he exerted his influence by addressing popular meetings, undergoing two years' imprisonment for a speech delivered at a Manchester meeting in 1819   After several unsuccessful attempts to enter Parliament, he was elected in 1831, but held his seat only two years, when, becoming estranged from the other Radical leaders, he retired from politics — ED.

in BURDETT; and he was perfectly right. I most sincerely hope, that my countrymen will finally destroy the tyrants who oppress them; but, I am very sure, that, before they succeed in it, they must cure themselves of the folly of depending for assistance on the *nobles* or the *half-nobles.*

After witnessing this conduct in Burdett, I set off home, and thought no more about effecting a Reform. The *Acts* that soon followed were, by me, looked upon as *matters of course.*[*] The tyranny could go on no longer *under disguise.* It was compelled to shew its naked face; but, it is now, in reality, not worse than it was before. It now does no more than rob the people, and that it did before. It kills more now out-right; but, men may as well be shot, or stabbed or hanged, as starved to death.

During the Spring and the early part of the Summer, of 1817, I made preparations for the departure of myself and family, and when all was ready, I bid an everlasting adieu to Boroughmongers, Sinecure placemen and place-women, pensioned Lords and Ladies, Standing Armies in time of peace, and (rejoice, oh! my children!) to a hireling, tithe-devouring Priesthood. We arrived safe and all in good health, and which health has never been impaired

---

[*] December 2, 1816, a large mob collected at Spa-fields, London, and after addresses by certain Radicals and Spencean Philanthropists (members of a society which aimed to abolish private property), it proceeded to take possession of the Tower, but disbanded before much damage had been done. Feeling confident that sedition was being plotted in all the newly-organized clubs throughout England, Parliament (March 3, 1817) authorized the suspension of the writ of habeas corpus March 25, the Seditious Meetings Act was passed, prescribing the death penalty for refusal to discontinue any meeting when required to do so by a magistrate (see *Parliamentary Debates*, xxxv, pp. 795, 826, 1083, 1227). The reformers regarded these laws as subversive of all liberty; Cobbett headed the articles in his *Register*, "A History of the Last Hundred Days of English Freedom, ending with the passing of the Absolute-Power-of-Imprisonment Act, in the Month of March, 1817 "— ED.

by the climate.   We are in a state of ease, safety, plenty; and how can we help being as happy as people can be? The more I see of my adopted country, the more gratitude do I feel towards it for affording me and my numerous offspring protection from the tyrants of my native country.   There I should have been in constant anxiety about my family.   Here I am in none at all.   Here I [268] am in fear of no *spies*, no *false witnesses*, no *blood-money men*. Here no fines, irons, or gallowses await me, let me *think* or *say* what I will about the government.   Here I have to pay no people to be ready to shoot at me, or run me through the body, or chop me down.   Here no vile Priest can rob me and mock me in the same breath.

In the year 1816 my travelling in America was confined to the Atlantic States.   I there saw enough to determine the question of emigration or no emigration. But, a spot *to settle on myself* was another matter; for, though I do not know, that I shall meddle with any sort of trade, or occupation, in the view of getting money, I ought to look about me, and to consider soberly as to a spot to *settle on* with so large a family.   It was right, therefore, for me to see the *Western Countries.*   I have done this; and the particulars, which I thought worthy my notice, I noted down in a *Journal.*   This Journal I now submit to the public.   My chief motive in the publication is to endeavour to convey useful information, and especially to those persons, who may be disposed to follow my example, and to withdraw their families and fortunes from beneath the hoofs of the tyrants of England.

I have not the vanity to suppose myself *eminently* qualified for any thing beyond my own profession; but I have been an attentive observer; I have raised a considerable fortune by my own industry and economy; I have, all my life long, studied the matters connected with agriculture, trade, and manufactures. I had a desire to acquire an accurate knowledge of the Western countries, and what I did acquire I have endeavoured to communicate to others. It was not my object to give flowery descriptions. I leave that to poets and painters. Neither have I attempted any *general* estimate of the means or manner of living, or getting money, in the West. But, I have contented myself with merely noting down the facts that struck me; and from those facts the reader must draw his conclusions.

In one respect I am a proper person to give an account of the Western Countries. I have *no lands there*: I have no *interest* there: I have nothing to warp [269] my judgment in favour of those countries: and yet, I have as little in the Atlantic States to warp my judgment in their favour. I am perfectly impartial in my feelings, and am, therefore, likely to be impartial in my words. My good wishes extend to the utmost boundary of my adopted country. Every particular part of it is as dear to me as every other particular part.

I have recommended most strenuously the encouraging and promoting of *Domestic Manufacture*; not because I mean to be engaged in any such concern myself; for it is by no means likely that I ever shall; but, because I think that such encouragement and promotion would be greatly beneficial to America, and because it would provide a happy Asylum for my native, oppressed, and distressed countrymen, who have been employed all the days of their lives in manufactures in England, where the principal part of the immense profits of their labour is consumed by the Borough tyrants and their friends, and expended for the vile purpose of perpetuating a system of plunder and despotism at home, and all over the world.

Before I conclude this Introduction, I must observe, that I see with great pain, and with some degree of shame, the behaviour of some persons from England, who, appear to think that they give proof of their *high breeding* by re-paying civility, kindness, and hospitality, with *reproach and insolence.* However, these persons are *despised.* They produce very little impression here; and, though the accounts they send to England, may be believed by some, they will have little effect on persons of sense and virtue. *Truth* will make its way; and it is, thank God, now making its way with great rapidity.

I could mention numerous instances of Englishmen, coming to this country with hardly a dollar in their pocket, and arriving at a state of ease and plenty and even riches in a few years; and I explicitly declare, that I have never known or heard of, an instance of one common labourer who, with common industry and economy, did not greatly better his lot. Indeed, how can it otherwise be, when the average wages of [270] agricultural labour is *double* what it is in England, and when the average price of food is not more than half what it is in that country? These two facts, undeniable as they are, are quite suffi-cient to satisfy any man of sound mind.

As to the *manners* of the people, they are precisely to my taste, unostentatious and simple. Good sense I find every where, and never affectation. Kindness, hospital-ity and never-failing civility. I have travelled more than four thousand miles about this country; and I have never met with one single insolent or rude native American.

I trouble myself very little about the party politics of the country. These contests are the natural offspring of freedom; and they tend to perpetuate that which produces them. I look at the people as a *whole*; and I love them and feel grateful to them for having given the world a practical proof, that peace, social order, and general happiness can be secured, and best secured, without Monarchs, Dukes, Counts, Baronets, and Knights. I have no unfriendly feeling towards any Religious Society. I wish well to every member of every such society; but, I love the Quakers, and feel grateful towards them, for having proved to the world, that all the virtues, public as well as private, flourish most and bring forth the fairest fruits when unincumbered with those noxious weeds. hireling priests.

THOMAS HULME

PITTSBURGH, *June* 3.— Arrived here with a friend as travelling companion, by the mail stage from Philadelphia, after a journey of six days; having set out on the 28th May.[1] We were much pleased with the face of the country, the greatest part of which was new to me. The route, as far as Lancaster, lay through a rich and fertile country, well cultivated by good, settled proprietors; the road excellent: smooth as the smoothest in England, and hard as those made by the cruel *corvées* in France. The country finer, but the road not always so good, all the way from Lancaster, by Little York, to Chambersburgh; after which it changes for mountains and poverty, except in timber. Chambersburgh is situated on the North West side of that fine valley which lies between the South and North Mountains, and which extends from beyond the North East boundary of Pennsylvania to nearly the South West extremity of North Carolina, and which has limestone for its bottom and rich and fertile soil, and beauty upon the face of it, from one end to the other. The ridges of mountains called the Allegany, and forming the highest land in north America between the Atlantic and Pacific oceans, begin here and extend across our route nearly 100 miles, or rather, *three days,* for it was no less than half the journey to travel over them; they rise one above the other as we proceed Westward, till we reach the Allegany, the last

---

[1] For a description of this route through western Pennsylvania at the beginning of the century, see F. A. Michaux's *Travels*, volume iii of our series, pp 132-156 — ED.

and most lofty of all, from which we have a view to the West farther than the eye can carry. I can say nothing in commendation of the road over these mountains, but I must admire the drivers, and their excellent horses. The road is every thing that is bad, but the skill of the drivers, and the well constructed vehicles, and the capital old English horses, overcome [272] every thing. We were rather singularly fortunate in not breaking down or up-setting; I certainly should not have been surprized if the whole thing, horses and all, had gone off the road and been dashed to pieces. A new road is making, however, and when that is completed, the journey will be shorter in point of time, just one half.[8] A fine even country we get into immediately on descending the Allegany, with very little appearance of unevenness or of barrenness all the way to Pittsburgh; the evidence of good land in the crops, and the country beautified by a various mixture of woods and fields.

Very good accommodations for travellers the whole of the way. The stage stops to breakfast and to dine, and sleeps where it sups. They literally feasted us every where, at every meal, with venison and good meat of all sorts: every thing in profusion. In one point, however, I must make an exception, with regard to some houses: at night I was surprized, in taverns so well kept in other respects, to find bugs in the beds! I am sorry to say I observed (or, rather, *felt*,) this too often. Always good eating and drinking, but not always good sleeping.

June 4th & *5th.*— Took a view of Pittsburgh. It is situated between the mouths of the river Allegany and Monongahela, at the point where they meet and begin

---

[8] For the Cumberland Road, see Harris's *Journal,* volume iii of our series, note 45.— Ed.

the Ohio, and is laid out in a triangular form so that two sides of it lie contiguous to the water. Called upon Mr. Bakewell, to whom we were introduced by letter, and who very obligingly satisfied our curiosity to see every thing of importance. After showing us through his extensive and well conducted glass works,[9] he rowed us across the Monongahela to see the mines from which the fine coals we had seen burning were brought. These coals are taken out from the side of a steep hill, very near to the river, and brought from thence and laid down in any part of the town for 7 cents the bushel, weighing, perhaps, 80lb. Better coals I never saw. A bridge is now building over the river, by which they will most probably be brought still cheaper.

This place surpasses even my expectations, both in natural resources and in extent of manufactures. [273] Here are the materials for every species of manufacture, nearly, and of excellent quality and in profusion; and these means have been taken advantage of by skilful and industrious artizans and mechanics from all parts of the world. There is scarcely a denomination of manufacture or manual profession that is not carried on to a great extent, and, as far as I have been able to examine, in the best manner. The manufacture of iron in all the different branches, and the mills of all sorts, which I examined with the most attention, are admirable.

Price of flour, from 4 to 5 dollars a barrel; butter 14 cents per lb.; other provisions in proportion and mechanic's and good labourer's wages 1 dollar, and shipbuilder's 1 dollar and a half, a day.

---

[9] The glassworks of Bakewell, Pears and Company were established in 1808. For the beginning of this industry in Pittsburg, see Cuming's *Tour*, volume iv of our series, note 28 — ED.

June 6th.— Leave Pittsburgh, and set out in a thing called an ark, which we buy for the purpose, down the Ohio.[10]   We have, besides, a small skiff, to tow the ark and go ashore occasionally.   This ark, which would stow away eight persons, close packed, is a thing by no means pleasant to travel in, especially at night.   It is strong at bottom, but may be compared to an orange-box, bowed over at top, and so badly made as to admit a boy's hand to steal the oranges: it is proof against the river, but not against the rain.

. Just on going to push off the wharf, an English officer stepped on board of us, with all the curiosity imaginable. I at once took him for a spy hired to way-lay travellers. He began a talk about the Western Countries, anxiously assuring us that we need not hope to meet with such a thing as a respectable person, travel where we would. I told him I hoped in God I should see no spy or informer, whether in plain clothes or regimentals, and that of one thing I was certain, at any rate: that I should find no Sinecure placeman or pensioner in the Western country.

The Ohio, at its commencement, is about 600 yards broad, and continues running with nearly parallel sides, taking two or three different directions in its course, for about 200 miles.   There is a curious contrast between the waters which form this river: that of the Allegany is clear and transparent, that of the Monongahela [274] thick and muddy, and it is not for a considerable distance that they entirely mingle.   The sides of the river are beautiful; there are always rich bottom lands upon the banks, which are steep and pretty high, varying in width

---

[10] See Harris's *Journal*, volume III of our series, p. 335, for a description of an Ohio River "ark."— ED.

from a few yards to a mile, and skirted with steep hills varying also in height, overhanging with fine timber.

June 7th.— Floating down the Ohio, at the rate of four miles an hour. Lightning, thunder, rain and hail pelting in upon us. The hail-stones as large as English hazel-nuts. Stop at Steubenville all night. A nice place; has more stores than taverns, which is a good sign.[11]

June 8th.— Came to Wheeling at about 12 o'clock. It is a handsome place, and of considerable note. Stopped about an hour. Found flour to be about 4 to 5 dollars a barrel; fresh beef 4 to 6 cents per lb., and other things (the produce of the country) about the same proportion. Labourers' wages, 1 dollar a day. Fine coals here, and at Steubenville.

June 9th.— Two fine young men join us, one a carpenter and the other a saddler, from Washington, in a skiff that they had bought at Pittsburgh, and in which they are taking a journey of about 700 miles down the river. We allow them to tie their skiff to our ark, for which they very cheerfully assist us. Much diverted to see the nimbleness with which they go on shore sometimes with their rifles to shoot pigeons and squirrels. The whole expenses of these two young men in floating the 700 miles, will be but 7 dollars each, including skiff and every thing else.

This day pass Marietta, a good looking town at the mouth of the Muskingham River. It is, however, like many other towns on the Ohio, built on too low ground, and is subject to inundations   Here I observe a contri-

---

[11] For the towns along the Ohio mentioned by Hulme, see A. Michaux's *Travels*, volume iii of our series: Wheeling, note 15, Marietta, note 16 Cuming's *Tour*, volume iv of our series   Steubenville, note 67; Cincinnati, note 166; Shippingport, note 171   Bradbury's *Travels*, volume v of our series, Vevay, note 164.   Croghan's *Journals*, volume i of our series: Louisville, note 106.— Ed

vance of great ingenuity. There is a stronge rope put across the mouth of the river, opposite the town, fastened to trees or large posts on each side; upon this rope runs a pulley or block, to which is attached a rope, and to the rope a ferry-boat, which, by moving the helm first one way and then the other, is propelled by the force of the water across the river backwards or forwards.

[275] *June 10th.*— Pass several fine coal mines, which like those at Pittsburgh, Steubenville, Wheeling and other places, are not above 50 yards from the river and are upwards of 10 yards above high water. The river now becomes more winding than we have hitherto found it. It is sometimes so serpentine that it appears before and behind like a continuation of lakes, and the hills on its banks seem to be the separations. Altogether, nothing can be more beautiful.

June 11th.— A very hot day, but I could not discover the degree of heat. On going along we bought two Perch, weighing about 8 lb. each, for 25 cents, of a boy who was fishing.[12] Fish of this sort will sometimes weigh 30 lbs. each.

June 12th.— Pass Portsmouth, at the mouth of the Scioto River. A sort of village, containing a hundred or two of houses. Not worthy of any particular remark.

June 13th.— Arrived at Cincinnati about midnight. Tied our ark to a large log at the side of the river, and went to sleep. Before morning, however, the fastening broke, and, if it had not been for a watchful back-woodsman whom we had taken on board some distance up the river, we might have floated ten or fifteen miles without knowing it. This back-woodsman, besides being of much service to us, has been a very entertaining com-

---

[12] The common American perch is the *Perca americana* or *flavescens.*— ED.

panion.   He says he has been in this country forty years, but that he is an Englishman, and was bred in Sherwood Forest (he could not have come from a better nursery). All his adventures he detailed to us very minutely, but dwelt with particular warmth upon one he had had with a priest, lately, who, to spite him for preaching, brought an action against him, but was cast and had to pay costs.

June 14th and 15th.— Called upon Doctor Drake [18] and upon a Mr. Bosson, to whom we had letters.   These gentlemen shewed us the greatest civility, and treated us with a sort of kindness which must have changed the opinion even of the English officer whom we saw at Pittsburgh, had he been with us.   I could tell that dirty hireling scout, that even in this short space of time, I have had the pleasure to meet many gentlemen, [276] very well informed, and possessing great knowledge as to their own country, evincing public spirit in all their actions, and hospitality and kindness in all their demeanour; but, if they be pensioners, male or female, or sinecure place lords or ladies, I have yet come across, thank God, no *respectable people.*

Cincinnati is a very fine town, and elegantly (not only in the American acceptation of the word) situated on the banks of the river, nearly opposite to Licking Creek, which runs out of Kentucky, and is a stream of considerable importance.   The country round the town is beautiful, and the soil rich; the fields in its immediate vicinity bear principally grass, and clover of different sorts, the fragrant smell of which perfumes the air.   The town itself ranks next to Pittsburgh, of the towns on the Ohio, in point of manufactures.

---

[18] For a brief biography of Dr. Drake, consult Flint's *Letters*, volume ix of our series, note 61.— Ed.

We sold our ark, and its produce formed a deduction from our expenses, which, with that deduction, amounted to 14 dollars each, including every thing, for the journey from Pittsburgh to this place, which is upwards of 500 miles. I could not but remark the price of fuel here; 2 dollars a cord for Hickory; a cord is 8 feet by 4, and 4 deep, and the wood, the best in the world; it burns much like green Ash, but gives more heat. This, which is of course the highest price for fuel in this part of the country, is only about a fifth of what it is at Philadelphia.

June 16th.— Left Cincinnati for Louisville with seven other persons, in a skiff about 20 feet long and 5 feet wide.

June 17th.— Stopped at VEVAY, a very neat and beautiful place, about 70 miles above the falls of the Ohio. Our visit here was principally to see the mode used, as well as what progress was made, in the cultivation of the vine, and I had a double curiosity, never having as yet seen a vineyard. These vineyards are cultivated entirely by a small settlement of Swiss, of about a dozen families, who have been here about ten years. They first settled on the Kentucky river, but did not succeed there. They plant the vines in rows, attached to stakes like espaliers, and they plough between with a one-horse plough. The grapes, [277] which are of the sorts of Claret and Madeira, look very fine and luxuriant, and will be ripe in about the middle of September. The soil and climate both appear to be quite congenial to the growth of the vine: the former rich and the latter warm. The north west wind, when it blows, is very cold, but the south, south east, and south west winds, which are always warm, are prevalent. The heat, in the middle of the summer, I understand, is very great, being generally above 85 degrees, and sometimes above 100 degrees. Each of these families has a

farm as well as a vineyard, so that they supply themselves
with almost every necessary and have their wine all clear
profit.   Their produce will this year be probably not
less than 5000 gallons; we bought 2 gallons of it at a dollar
each, as good as I would wish to drink.   Thus it is that
the tyrants of Europe create vineyards in this new country!

June 18th.— Arrived at Louisville, Kentucky.   The
town is situated at the commencement of the falls, or
rapids of the Ohio.   The river, at this place, is little less
than a mile wide, and the falls continue from a ledge of
rocks which runs across the river in a sloping direction at
this part, to Shippingport, about 2 miles lower down.
Perceiving stagnant waters about the town, and an appearance of the house that we stopped at being infested
with bugs, we resolved not to make any stay at Louisville,
but got into our skiff and floated down the falls to Shippingport.   We found it very rough floating, not to say
dangerous.   The river of very unequal widths and full of
islands and rocks along this short distance, and the cur-
rent very rapid, though the descent is not more than 22
feet.   At certain times of the year the water rises so that
there is no fall; large boats can then pass.

At Shippingport, stopped at the house of Mr. Berthoud,[14]
a very respectable French gentleman, from whom we received the greatest civility during our stay, which was two
nights and the day intervening.

Shippingport is situated at a place of very great importance, being the upper extremity of that part of the
river which is navigable for heavy steam-boats.   All the
goods coming from the country are re-shipped, and every

---

[14] James Berthoud in 1803 purchased the town of Shippingport from the
original proprietor, Colonel John Campbell — ED.

thing going to it is un-shipped, here. Mr. Berthoud [278] has the store in which the articles exporting or importing are lodged: and is, indeed, a great shipper, though at a thousand miles from the sea.

June 20th.— Left the good and comfortable house of Mr. Berthoud, very much pleased with him and his amiable wife and family, though I differed with him a little in politics. Having been taught at church, when a boy, that the Pope was the whore of Babylon, that the Bourbons were tyrants, and that the Priests and privileged orders of France were impostors and petty tyrants under them, I could not agree with him in applauding the Boroughmongers of England for re-subjugating the people of France, and restoring the Bourbons, the Pope, and the Inquisition.

Stop at New Albany, 2 miles below Shippingport, till the evening.[15] A Mr. Paxton, I am told, is the proprietor of a great part of the town, and has the grist and saw-mills, which are worked by steam, and the ferry across the river. Leave this place in company with a couple of young men from the western part of the state of New York, who are on their way to Tennessee in a small ferry-boat. Their whole journey will, probably, be about 1,500 miles.

June 21st.— Floating down the river, without any thing in particular occurring.

June 22nd.— Saw a Mr. Johnstone and his wife reaping wheat on the side of the river. They told us they had come to this spot last year, direct from Manchester,

---

[15] The site of New Albany was owned by three Scribner brothers of New York, who in 1813 had a town surveyed and offered lots for sale. In 1819 it contained about one hundred and fifty houses and a thousand inhabitants. Charles Paxson removed from Philadelphia (1817) and opened a store at New Albany. For many years he owned the only brick house in the village.— ED

Old England, and had bought their little farm of 55 acres of a back-woodsman who had cleared it, and was glad to move further westward, for 3 dollars an acre. They had a fine flock of little children, and pigs and poultry, and were cheerful and happy, being confident that their industry and economy would not be frustrated by visits for tithes or taxes.

June 23rd.—— See great quantities of turkey-buzzards and thousands of pigeons. Came to Pigeon Creek, about 230 miles below the Falls, and stopped for the night at Evansville, a town of nine months old, near the mouth of it.[16] We are now frequently met and passed by large, fine steam-boats, plying up and down [279] the river. One went by us as we arrived here which had left Shipping-port only the evening before. They go down the river at the rate of 10 miles an hour, and charge passengers 6 cents a mile, boarding and lodging included. The price is great, but the time is short.

June 24th.—— Left Evansville. This little place is rapidly increasing, and promises to be a town of consider-able trade. It is situated at a spot which seems likely to become a port for shipping to Princeton and a pretty large district of Indiana. I find that the land speculators have made entry of the most eligible tracts of land, which will impede the partial, though not the final, progress of population and improvement in this part of the state.

---

[16] The first log cabin on the site of Evansville was built in 1812 by Hugh McGary of Kentucky. Four years later General Robert Evans, having pur-chased the land in the vicinity, surveyed and laid out a town which he named Evansville. It did not attract settlers until 1818, when Evans succeeded in having it made the seat of the newly-erected Vanderburgh County. In 1819 it contained one hundred inhabitants; but Hulme's expectation of its future importance was slow in being realized, for in 1830 the population was but five hundred. It was incorporated in 1847, and from that date its growth has been rapid.—— ED.

On our way to Princeton, we see large flocks of fine wild turkeys, and whole herds of pigs, apparently very fat. The pigs are wild also, but have become so from neglect. Some of the inhabitants, who prefer sport to work, live by shooting these wild turkeys and pigs, and indeed, sometimes, I understand, they shoot and carry off those of their neighbours before they are wild.

June 25th.— Arrived at Princeton, Indiana, about twenty miles from the river.[17] ,I was sorry to see very little doing in this town. They cannot *all* keep stores and taverns! One of the storekeepers told me he does not sell more than ten thousand dollars value per annum: he ought, then, to manufacture something and not spend nine tenths of his time in lolling with a segar in his mouth.

June 26th.— At Princeton, endeavouring to purchase horses, as we had now gone far enough down the Ohio. While waiting in our tavern, two men called in armed with rifles, and made enquiries for some horses they suspected to be stolen. They told us they had been almost all the way from Albany, to Shawnee town [18] after them, a distance of about 150 miles. I asked them how they would be able to secure the thieves, if they overtook them, in these wild woods; "O," said they, "shoot them off the horses." This is a summary mode of executing justice, thought I, though probably the most effectual, and, indeed, only one in this state of society. A thief very

[17] As early as 1800 settlement began in the vicinity of the present town of Princeton. Gibson County being organized in 1813 and the county seat located there, the following year a public square was cleared of timber, and town lots were offered for sale. It was named in honor of William Prince, a lawyer and Indian agent who had settled at Princeton in 1812, he later became a circuit court judge and a member of Congress — ED

[18] For the founding of Shawneetown, see Croghan's *Journals*, volume i of our series, note 108.— ED

rarely escapes here; not nearly so [280] often as in more populous districts. The fact was, in this case, however, we discovered afterwards, that the horses had strayed away, and had returned home by this time. But, if they had been stolen, the stealers would not have escaped. When the loser is tired, another will take up the pursuit, and the whole country is up in arms till he is found.

June 27th.— Still at Princeton. At last we get suited with horses. Mine cost me only 135 dollars with the bridle and saddle, and that I am told is 18 dollars too much.

June 28th.— Left Princeton, and set out to see Mr. Birkbeck's settlement, in Illinois, about 35 miles from Princeton.[19] Before we got to the Wabash we had to cross a swamp of half a mile wide; we were obliged to lead our horses, and walk up to the knees in mud and water. Before we got half across we began to think of going back; but, there is a sound bottom under it all, and we waded through it as well as we could. It is, in fact, nothing but a bed of very soft and rich land, and only wants draining to be made productive. We soon after came to the banks of the great Wabash, which is

[19] Morris Birkbeck (1763-1825) was a native of England, being born at Wanborough He received a classical education and became a successful, practical farmer. Having become acquainted with a number of Americans, especially with Edward Coles, later governor of Illinois, Birkbeck emigrated (1817) to America. He purchased sixteen thousand acres in Illinois, upon which he located the widely known "English settlement" in Edwards County, whose chief town was Albion. Birkbeck and family settled a few miles distant, naming their point of residence Wanborough Having considerable literary ability, he assisted Governor Coles in the latter's fight against admitting slavery into Illinois In 1824 he was appointed secretary of state by Coles, but the senate, being pro-slavery, refused to confirm the nomination In 1825, while returning from a visit to the New Harmony settlement, Birkbeck was drowned in Fox River. He was the author of *Notes on a Journey Through France* (London, 1815), *Notes on a Journey in America* (London, 1818), and *Letters from Illinois* (London, 1818), and some controversial pamphlets.— ED

here about half a mile broad, and as the ferry-boat was crossing over with us I amused myself by washing my dirty boots. Before we mounted again we happened to meet with a neighbour of Mr. Birkbeck's, who was returning home; we accompanied him, and soon entered into the prairie lands, up to our horses' bellies in fine grass. These prairies, which are surrounded with lofty woods, put me in mind of immense noblemen's parks in England. Some of those we passed over are called *wet prairies*, but, they are dry at this time of the year; and, as they are none of them flat, they need but very simple draining to carry off the water all the year round. Our horses were very much tormented with flies, some as large as the English horse-fly and some as large as the wasp; these flies infest the prairies that are unimproved about three months in the year, but go away altogether as soon as cultivation begins.

Mr. Birkbeck's settlement is situated between [281] the two Wabashes, and is about ten miles from the nearest navigable water; we arrived there about sunset and met with a welcome which amply repaid us for our day's toil. We found that gentleman with his two sons perfectly healthy and in high spirits: his daughters were at Henderson (a town in Kentucky, on the Ohio) on a visit.[20] At present his habitation is a cabin, the building of which cost only 20 dollars; this little hutch is near the spot where he is about to build his house, which he intends to have in the most eligible situation in the prairie for

[20] Birkbeck brought four children with him to Illinois: his second son, Bradford, aged sixteen; his third son, Charles, aged fourteen; his daughter Eliza, who later married Gilbert Pell; and his daughter Prudence, who married Francis Hanks. Soon after their father's death, the family left Illinois, the two sons and Mrs Hanks going to Mexico, and Mrs. Pell to England to educate her children.— ED.

convenience to fuel and for shelter in winter, as well as for breezes in summer, and will, when that is completed, make one of its appurtenances. I like this plan of keeping the old loghouse; it reminds the grand children and their children's children of what their ancestor has done for their sake.

Few settlers had as yet joined Mr. Birkbeck; that is to say, settlers likely to become "*society*;" he has labourers enough near him, either in his own houses or on land of their own joining his estate. He was in daily expectation of his friends, Mr. Fowler's family,[21] however, with a large party besides; they had just landed at Shawnee Town, about 20 miles distant. Mr. Birkbeck informs me he has made entry of a large tract of land, lying, part of it, all the way from his residence to the great Wabash; this he will re-sell again in lots to any of his friends, they taking as much of it and wherever they choose (provided it be no more than they can cultivate), at an advance which I think very fair and liberal.

The whole of his operations had been directed hitherto (and wisely in my opinion) to building, fencing, and other

---

[21] George Flower, born about 1780, was an Englishman of means who emigrated to America in 1816 in search of the famed prairies of Illinois, of which so much was being said. Visiting the Middle West in that year, he returned to Virginia and spent the winter, chiefly with Thomas Jefferson, to whom he had letters of introduction from Lafayette. In 1817, Morris Birkbeck arrived, and, as the two were old friends, Flower joined Birkbeck's movement and took part in founding the "English settlement." In 1818, on returning from a voyage to England, Flower was accompanied by his father (Richard, who wrote the letters reprinted in this volume), his mother, two sisters, and two brothers. After spending the winter in Lexington, the newcomers of the family removed to English Prairie in the spring of 1819. George Flower championed the movement against admitting slavery into Illinois, and lived to see Albion become a prosperous and beautiful town. He was financially unfortunate, and for many years lived in retirement with his children in Illinois and Indiana. Shortly before his death (1862) he completed a *History of the English Settlement in Edwards County, Illinois* (Chicago, 1882).— ED

important preparations. He had done nothing in the cultivating way but make a good garden, which supplies him with the only things that he cannot purchase, and, at present, perhaps, with more economy than he could grow them. He is within twenty miles of Harmony;[22] in Indiana, where he gets his flour and all other necessaries (the produce of the country) and therefore employs himself much better in making barns and houses and mills for the reception and disposal of [282] his crops, and fences to preserve them while growing, *before he grows them*, than to *get the crops first*. I have heard it observed that *any* American settler, even without a dollar in his pocket, would have *had something growing by this time*. Very true! I do not question that at all; for, the very first care of a settler without a dollar in his pocket is to get something to eat, and, he would consequently set to work scratching up the earth, fully confident that after a long summering upon wild flesh (without salt, perhaps) his own belly would stand him for barn, if his jaws would not for mill. But the case is very different with Mr. Birkbeck, and at present he has need for no other provision for winter but about a three hundredth part of his fine grass turned into hay, which will keep his necessary horses and cows: besides which he has nothing that eats but

____

[22] Harmony (or Harmonie as it was first known) was the famous settlement of the German Lutherans led by George Rapp. In 1813 Rapp purchased thirty thousand acres along the Wabash, on a part of which New Harmony was built. "Contrary to the general idea, Rapp's colony was a great success, so far as the accumulation of property was concerned, and when Rapp sold out, in 1825, it was said the wealth per capita was ten times greater than the average wealth throughout the United States "— E B. Washburne, editorial note to Flower's *English Settlement in Edwards County, Illinois*, p 61. The town was purchased by Robert Owen, a manufacturer of New Lanark Scotland, for the purpose of putting into practice his communistic ideas. After a few years the communistic plan was abandoned, and Owen returned to Scotland, leaving the property in charge of his two sons — Ed

such pigs as live upon the waste, and a couple of fine young deer (which would weigh, they say, when full grown, 200 lb. dead weight) that his youngest son is rearing up as pets.

I very much admire Mr. Birkbeck's mode of *fencing*. He makes a ditch 4 feet wide at top, sloping to 1 foot wide at bottom, and 4 feet deep. With the earth that comes out of the ditch he makes a bank on one side, which is turfed towards the ditch. Then a long pole is put up from the bottom of the ditch to 2 feet above the bank; this is crossed by a short pole from the other side, and then a rail is laid along between the forks. The banks were growing beautifully, and looked altogether very neat as well as formidable; though a live hedge (which he intends to have) instead of dead poles and rails, upon top, would make the fence far more effectual as well as handsomer. I am always surprised, until I reflect how universally and to what a degree, farming is neglected in this country, that this mode of fencing is not adopted in cultivated districts, especially where the land is wet, or lies low; for, there it answers a double purpose, being as effectual a drain as it is a fence.

I was rather disappointed, or sorry, at any rate, not to find near Mr. Birkbeck's any of the means for machinery or of the materials for manufactures, such as the water-falls, and the minerals and mines, [283] which are possessed in such abundance by the states of Ohio and Kentucky, and by some parts of Pennsylvania. Some of these, however, he may yet find. Good water he has, at any rate. He showed me a well 25 feet deep, bored partly through hard substances near the bottom, that was nearly overflowing with water of excellent quality.

July 1st.— Left Mr. Birkbeck's for Harmony, Indiana.

The distance by the direct way is about 18 miles, but, there is no road, as yet; indeed, it was often with much difficulty that we could discover the way at all. After we had crossed the Wabash, which we did at a place called Davis's Ferry,[23] we hired a man to conduct us some part of the way through the woods. In about a mile he brought us to a track, which was marked out by slips of bark being stripped off the trees, once in about 40 yards; he then left us and told us we could not mistake if we followed that track. We soon lost all appearance of the track, however, and of the "*blazing*" of the trees, as they call it; but, as it was useless to go back again for another guide, our only way was to keep straight on in the same direction, bring us where it would. Having no compass, this nearly cost us our sight, for it was just mid-day, and we had to gaze at the sun a long time before we discovered what was our course. After this we soon, to our great joy, found ourselves in a large corn field; rode round it, and came to Johnson's Ferry, a place where a Bayou (*Boyau*) of the Wabash is crossed. This Bayou is a run out of the main river round a flat portion of land, which is sometimes overflowed: it is part of the same river, and the land encompassed by it, an island. Crossed this ferry in a canoe, and got a ferry-man to swim our horses after us. Mounted again and followed a track which brought us to Black River, which we forded without getting wet, by holding our feet up.[24] After crossing the river we found a man who was kind enough to shew us about half a mile through the woods, by which our journey was shortened five or six miles. He put us into a direct track to Har-

---

[23] Davis's ferry across the Wabash was twelve miles from Albion.— ED.

[24] Black River, or Creek, rises in the southern part of Gibson County, Indiana, and flows westward, emptying into the Wabash a few miles above New Harmony.— ED.

mony, through lands as rich as a dung-hill, and covered with immense timber; we [284] thanked him, and pushed on our horses with eager curiosity to see this far-famed Harmonist Society.

On coming within the precincts of the Harmonites we found ourselves at the side of the Wabash again; the river on our right hand, and their lands on our left.   Our road now lay across a field of Indian corn, of, at the very least, a mile in width, and bordering the town on the side we entered; I wanted nothing more than to behold this immense field of most beautiful corn to be at once convinced of all I had heard of the industry of this society of Germans, and I found, on proceeding a little farther, that the progress they had made exceeded all my idea of it.

The town is methodically laid out in a situation well chosen in all respects; the houses are good and clean, and have, each one, a nice garden well stocked with all vegetables and tastily ornamented with flowers.   I observe that these people are very fond of flowers, by the bye; the cultivation of them, and musick, are their chief amusements.   I am sorry to see this, as it is to me a strong symptom of simplicity and ignorance, if not a badge of their German slavery.   Perhaps the pains they take with them is the cause of their flowers being finer than any I have hitherto seen in America, but, most probably, the climate here is more favourable.   Having refreshed ourselves at the Tavern, where we found every thing we wanted for ourselves and our horses, and all very clean and nice, besides many good things we did not expect, such as beer, porter, and even wine, all made within the Society, and very good indeed, we then went out to see the people at their harvest, which was just begun.   There were 150 men and women all reaping in the same field of wheat. A beautiful sight! The crop was very fine, and the field, extending to about two miles in length, and from half a mile to a mile in width, was all open to one view, the sun shining on it from the West, and the reapers advancing regularly over it.

At sun-set all the people came in, from the fields, workshops, mills, manufactories, and from all their labours. This being their evening for prayer [285] during the week, the Church bell called them out again in about 15 minutes, to attend a lecture from their High Priest and Law-giver, Mr. George Rapp.[25] We went to hear the lecture, or, rather, to see the performance, for, it being all performed in German, we could understand not a word. The people were all collected in a twinkling, the men at one end of the Church and the women at the other; it looked something like a Quaker Meeting, except that there was not a single little child in the place. Here they were kept by their Pastor a couple of hours, after which they returned home to bed. This is the quantum of Church-service they perform during the week; but on Sundays they are in Church nearly the whole of the time from getting up to going to bed. When it happens that Mr. Rapp cannot attend, either by indisposition or other accident, the Society still meet as usual, and the *elders* (certain of the most trusty and discreet, whom the Pastor selects as a sort of assistants

[25] George Rapp (1757-1847) was a weaver in Iptingen, Wurtemburg, and was noted for his biblical knowledge and piety. He proposed to reform society on the plan of the New Testament, gathering around him a community of persons who, in imitation of the early Christians at Jerusalem, held everything in common. This brought them into disfavor with the government, and he, with a portion of his followers, emigrated to the United States (1803), settling first on Conequenessing Creek, Butler County, Pennsylvania In 1815, he established Harmony, on the Wabash, but ten years later led the colony back to Pennsylvania, and founded the town of Economy, about seventeen miles northwest of Pittsburg See also, note 22, *ante* — ED.

in his divine commission) converse on religious subjects.

Return to the Tavern to sleep; a good comfortable house, well kept by decent people, and the master himself, who is very intelligent and obliging, is one of the very few at Harmony who can speak English. Our beds were as good as those stretched upon by the most highly pensioned and placed Boroughmongers, and our sleep, I hope, much better than the tyrants ever get, in spite of all their dungeons and gags.

July 2nd.— Early in the morning, took a look at the manufacturing establishment, accompanied by our Tavern-keeper. I find great attention is paid to this branch of their affairs. Their principle is, not to be content with the profit upon the manual labour of *raising* the article, but also to have the benefit of the machine in preparing it for *use.* I agree with them perfectly, and only wish the subject was as well understood all over the United States as it is at Harmony. It is to their skill in this way that they owe their great prosperity; if they had been nothing but farmers, they would be now at Harmony in Pennsylvania, poor cultivators, getting a bare subsistence, instead of having doubled their property two or three [286] times over, by which they have been able to move here and select one of the choicest spots in the country.

But in noting down the state of this Society, as it now is, its *origin* should not be forgotten; the curious history of it serves as an explanation to the jumble of sense and absurdity in the association. I will therefore trace the Harmonist Society from its outset in Germany to this place.

The Sect had its origin at Wurtemberg in Germany, about 40 years ago, in the person of its present Pastor and Master, George Rapp, who, by his own account, "having long seen and felt the decline of the Church, found himself impelled to bear testimony to the fundamental principles of the Christian Religion; and, finding no toleration for his inspired doctrines, or for those who adopted them, he determined with his followers to go to that part of the earth, where they were free to worship God according to the dictates of their conscience." In other words (I suppose), he had long beheld and experienced the slavery and misery of his country, and, feeling in his conscience that he was born more for a ruler than for a slave, found himself imperiously called upon to collect together a body of his poor countrymen and to lead them into a land of liberty and abundance. However allowing him to have had no other than his professed views, he, after he had got a considerable number of proselytes, amounting to seven or eight hundred persons, among whom were a sufficiency of good labourers and artizans in all the essential branches of workmanship and trade, besides farmers, he embodied them into a Society, and then came himself to America (not trusting to Providence to lead the way) to seek out the land destined for these chosen children. Having done so, and laid the plan for his route to the land of peace and Christian love, with a foresight which shows him to have been by no means unmindful to the *temporal* prosperity of the Society, he then landed his followers in separate bodies, and prudently led them in that order to a resting place within Pennsylvania, choosing rather to retard their progress through the wilderness than to hazard the discontent that might arise from want and fatigue [287] in traversing it at once. When they were all arrived, Rapp constituted them into one body, having every thing in common, and called the settlement *Harmony*. This constitution he found authorised by the passage in Acts, iv. 32, ''And the multitude of them that believed were ·

of one heart, and of one soul: neither said any of them that aught of the things he possessed was his own, *but that they had all things common.*" Being thus associated, the Society went to work, early in 1805, building houses and clearing lands, according to the order and regulations of their leader; but the community of stock, or the regular discipline, or the restraints which he had reduced them to, and which were essential to his project, soon began to thin his followers and principally, too, those of them who had brought most substance into the society, they demanded back their original portions and set out to seek the Lord by themselves. This falling off of the society, though it was but small, comparatively, in point of numbers, was a great reduction from their means; they had calculated what they should want to consume, and had laid the rest out in land; so that the remaining part were subjected to great hardships and difficulties for the first year or two of their settling, which was during the time of their greatest labours. However, it was not long before they began to reap the fruits of their toil, and in the space of six or seven years their settlement became a most flourishing colony. During that short space of time they brought into cultivation 3,000 acres of land (a third of their whole estate), reared a flock of nearly 2,000 sheep, and planted hop-gardens, orchards, and vineyards; built barns and stables to house their crops and their live stock, granaries to keep one year's produce of grain always in advance, houses to make their cyder, beer, and wine in, and good brick or stone warehouses for their several species of goods; constructed distilleries, mills for grinding, sawing, making oil, and, indeed, for every purpose, and machines for manufacturing their various materials for clothing and other uses; they had, besides, a store for retailing Philadelphia goods to the country, and nearly 100 good dwelling-houses of wood, a large stone-built tavern, [288] and, as a proof of superabundance, a dwelling-house and a meeting-house (alias the parsonage and church) which they had neatly built of brick.   And, besides all these improvements within the society, they did a great deal of business, principally in the way of manufacturing, for the people of the country. They worked for them with their mills and machines, some of which did nothing else, and their blacksmiths, tailors, shoe-makers, &c. when not employed by themselves, were constantly at work for their neighbours.   Thus this everlastingly-at-work band of emigrants increased their stock before they quitted their first colony, to upwards of two hundred thousand dollars, from, probably not one fifth of that sum.   What will not unceasing perseverance accomplish?   But, with judgment and order to direct it, what in the world can stand against it![26]

In comparing the state of this society as it now is with what it was in Pennsylvania, it is just the same as to *plan*; the temporal and spiritual affairs are managed in the same way, and upon the same principles, only both are more flourishing.   Rapp has here brought his disciples into richer land, and into a situation better in every respect, both for carrying on their trade, and for keeping to their faith; their vast extent of land is, they say, four feet deep of rich mould, nearly the whole of it, and it lies along the banks of a fine navigable river on one side, while the possibility of much interruption from other classes of Christians is effectually guarded against by an endless barricado of woods on the other side.   Bringing the means and experience acquired at their first establishment, they have

---

[26] A more detailed account of this society, up to the year 1811, will be found in Mr Mellishe's *Travels*, volume ii.— HULME

of course gone on improving and increasing (not in *popu-lation*) at a much greater rate. One of their greatest improvements, they tell me is the working of their mills and manufacturing machines by steam; they feel the advantage of this more and more every year. They are now preparing to build a steam boat; this is to be employed in their traffick with New Orleans [289] carrying their own surplus produce and returning with tea, coffee, and other commodities for their own consumption, and to retail to the people of the country. I believe they advance, too, in the way of ornaments and superfluities, for the dwelling-house they have now built their pastor, more resembles a Bishop's Palace than what I should figure to myself as the humble abode of a teacher of the "fundamental principles of the Christian Religion."

The government of this society is by bands, each consisting of a distinct trade or calling. They have a foreman to each band, who rules it under the general direction of the society, the law-giving power of which is in the High Priest. He cannot, however make laws without the consent of the parties. The manufacturing establishment, and the mercantile affairs and public accounts are all managed by one person; he, I believe, is one of the sons of Rapp. They have a bank, where a separate account is kept for each person; if any one puts in money, or has put in money, he may on certain conditions as to time, take it out again. They labour and possess in common; that is to say, except where it is not practicable or is immaterial, as with their houses, gardens, cows and poultry, which they have to themselves, each family. They also retain what property each may bring on joining the concern, and he may demand it in case of leaving the society, but *without interest*.

Here is certainly a wonderful example of the effects of skill, industry, and force combined. This congregation of far-seeing, ingenious, crafty, and bold, and of ignorant, simple, superstitious, and obedient, Germans, has shown what may be done. But their example, I believe, will generally only tend to confirm this free people in their suspicion that labour is concomitant to slavery or ignorance. Instead of their improvements, and their success and prosperity altogether, producing admiration, if not envy, they have a social discipline, the thought of which reduces these feelings to ridicule and contempt: that is to say, with regard to the *mass*; with respect to their leaders one's feelings are apt to be stronger. A fundamental of their religious creed (*"restraining* [290] *clause,"* a Chancery Lawyer would call it) requires restrictions on the propagation of the species; it orders such regulations as are necessary to prevent children coming but once in a certain number of years; and this matter is so arranged that, when they come, they come in little flocks, all within the same month, perhaps, like a farmer's lambs. The Law-giver here made a famously "restraining statute" upon the law of nature! This way of expounding law seems to be a main point of his policy; he by this means keeps his associates from increasing to an unruly number within, while more are sure not to come in from without; and, I really am afraid he will go a good way towards securing a monopoly of many great improvements in agriculture, both as to principle and method. People see the fine fields of the Harmonites, but, the prospect comes damped with the idea of bondage and celibacy. It is a curious society: was ever one heard of before that did not wish to increase! This smells strong of policy; some distinct view in the leaders, no doubt. Who would be surprised if we were to see a still more curious society by and bye ? A *Society Sole*! very far from improbable, if the sons of Rapp (for he has children, nevertheless, as well as Parson Malthus)[27] and the *Elders* were to die, it not being likely that they will renounce or forfeit their right to the common stock. We should then have societies as well as corporations vested in one person! That would be quite a novel kind of benefice! but, not the less fat. I question whether the *associated* person of Mr. Rapp would not be in possession of as fine a domain and as many good things as the *incorporated* person of an Archbishop: nay, he would rival the Pope! But, to my journal.

Arrive at Princeton in the evening; a good part of our road lay over the fine lands of the Harmonites. I understand, by the bye, that the title deeds to these lands are taken in the name of *Rapp and of his associates*. Poor associates: if they do but 'rebel! Find the same storekeepers and tavern-keepers in the same attitudes that we left them in the other day. Their legs *only a little* higher than their heads, and [291] segars in their mouths; a fine position for business! It puts my friend in mind of the Roman posture in dining.

July 3rd.— At Princeton all day. This is a pretty considerable place; very good as to buildings; but is too much inland to be a town of any consequence until the inhabitants do that at home which they employ merchants and foreign manufacturers to do for them. Pay 1 dollar for a set of old shoes to my horse, half the price of new ones.

---

[27] Robert Malthus (1766-1834), an English economist, who held the theory that the increase of population is more rapid than the increase of the means of subsistence, and consequently must be held in check, was himself a married man and had a son and daughter. Earlier in life he had held a curacy; the title "Parson Malthus" was sneeringly given to him by Cobbett, as his later doctrines were considered unsuitable for a clergyman.— ED.

July 4th.—Leave Princeton; in the evening, reach a place very appropriately called Mud-holes,[28] after riding 46 miles over lands in general very good but very little cultivated, and that little very badly; the latter part of the journey in company with a Mr. Jones from Kentucky. Nature is the agriculturist here; speculation instead of cultivation, is the order of the day amongst men. We feel the ill effects of this in the difficulty of getting oats for our horses. However, the evil is unavoidable, if it can be really called an evil. As well might I grumble that farmers have not taken possession as complain that men of capital have. Labour is the thing wanted, but, to have that money must come first. This Mud-holes was a sort of fort, not 4 years ago, for guarding against the Indians, who then committed great depredations, killing whole families often, men, women and children. How changeable are the affairs of this world! I have not met with a single Indian in the whole course of my route.

July 5th.— Come to Judge Chambers's,[29] a good tavern; 35 miles. On our way, pass French Lick, a strong spring of water impregnated with salt and sulphur, and called *Lick* from its being resorted to by cattle for the salt; close by this spring is another still larger, of fine clear lime-

---

[28] "Mud-holes" was located near the White River, in the northwestern part of the present Du Bois County It was on an old trail called "Mud-hole trace," which led from Vincennes to Jeffersonville. As early as 1802, before the land had been ceded by the Indians, two McDonald brothers from Virginia settled there. They were soon followed by other pioneers, and a blockhouse was built as a refuge in case of an Indian attack.— ED.

[29] This is now Chambersburg, in Orange County, about thirty-eight miles northwest of New Albany. It was named in honor of Samuel Chambers, who emigrated from North Carolina (1811) and established the first store and tavern at this place. When Orange County was organized (1816), he was appointed a county judge — ED.

stone water, running fast enough to turn a mill.[30]   Some of the trees near the Judge's exhibit a curious spectacle; a large piece of wood appears totally dead, all the leaves brown and the branches broken, from being roosted upon lately by an enormous multitude of pigeons.   A novel sight for us, unaccustomed to the abundance of the back-woods! [292] No tavern but this, nor house of any description, within many miles.

July 6th.— Leave the Judge's, still in company with Mr. Jones.   Ride 25 miles to breakfast, not sooner finding feed for our horses; this was at the dirty log-house of Mr.———— who has a large farm with a grist-mill on it, and keeps his yard and stables ancle deep in mud and water.   If this were not one of the healthiest climates in the world, he and his family must have died in all this filth.   About 13 miles further, come to New Albany, where we stop at Mr. Jenkins's, the best tavern we have found in Indiana, that at Harmony excepted.

July 7th.— Resting at New Albany.   We were amused by hearing a Quaker-lady preach to the natives.   Her first words were "*All the nations of the earth are of one blood.*" "So," said I to myself, "this question, which has so long perplexed philosophers, divines and physicians, is now set at rest!"   She proceeded to vent her rage with great vehemence against hireling priests and the trade of preach-ing in general, and closed with dealing out large portions of brimstone to the drunkard and still larger and hotter to those who give the bottle to drink.   This part of her discourse pleased me very much and may be a saving to

[30] French Lick is about fifty miles northwest of New Albany   The springs were donated to the state by Congress on the supposition that salt could profit-ably be manufactured therefrom, but this did not prove practicable.   In recent years French Lick and West Baden Springs, a half-mile distant, have won attention as health resorts.— ED.

me into the bargain; for, the dread of everlasting roasting added to my love of economy will (I think) prevent me making my friends tipsy. A very efficacious sermon!

July 8th.— Jenkins's is a good tavern, but it entertains at a high price. Our bill was 6 dollars each for a day and two nights; a shameful charge. Leave New Albany, cross the Ohio, and pass through Louisville in Kentucky again, on our way to Lexington, the capital. Stop for the night at Mr. Netherton's, a good tavern. The land hitherto is good, and the country altogether healthy, if I may judge from the people who appear more cheerful and happy than in Indiana, always excepting Harmony. Our land-lord is the picture of health and strength: 6 feet 4 inches high, weighs 300lb. and not fat.

July 9th.— Dine at Mr. Overton's tavern, on our way to Frankfort; pay half a dollar each for an excellent dinner, with as much brandy and butter-milk [293] as we choose to drink, and good feed for our horses. In the afternoon we have the pleasure to be overtaken by two ladies on horseback, and have their agreeable company for a mile or two. On their turning off from our road we were very reluctantly obliged to refuse an obliging invitation to drink tea at their house, and myself the more so, as one of the ladies informed me she had married a Mr. Constantine, a gentleman from my own native town of Bolton, in Lancashire. But, we had yet so far to go, and it was getting dark. This most healthful mode of travelling is universal in the Western States, and it gives me great pleasure to see it; though, perhaps, I have to thank the badness of the roads as the cause. Arrive at Frankfort, apparently a thriving town, on the side of the rough Kentucky river.[31] The houses are built chiefly of brick, and the streets, I

---

[31] For the early history of Frankfort, see F. A. Michaux's *Travels*, volume iii of our series, note 39 — ED

understand, paved with limestone. Limestone abounds in this state, and yet the roads are not good, though better than in Indiana and Ohio, for there there are none. I wonder the government of these states do not set about making good roads and bridges, and even canals [32] I pledge myself to be able to shew them how the money might be raised, and, moreover, to prove that the expense would be paid over and over again in almost no time. Such improvements would be income to the governments instead of expense, besides being such an incalculable benefit to the states. But, at any rate, why not *roads*, and in *this* state, too, which is so remarkable for its quality of having good road materials and rich land together, generally all over it?

July 10th.—Leave Frankfort, and come through a district of fine land, very well watered, to Lexington; stop at Mr. Keen's tavern. Had the good fortune to meet Mr. Clay, who carried us to his house, about a mile in the country.[33] It is a beautiful residence, situated near the centre of a very fine farm, which is just cleared and is coming into excellent cultivation. I approve of Mr. Clay's method very much, especially in laying down pasture. He clears away all the brush or underwood, leaving timber enough to afford a sufficiency of shade to the grass, which does not thrive here exposed [294] to the sun as in England

---

[32] The first macadamized road in Kentucky, and the first to receive state aid, was the Maysville and Lexington turnpike. It was begun in 1829, the state subscribing for $25,000 worth of stock. Congress, also, voted to subscribe for fifteen hundred shares; but the now famous Maysville Road Bill was vetoed by President Jackson The state then made further contributions amounting to half the cost of the road A great interest in road building was now aroused, by November, 1837, 343 miles of macadamized road had been completed with the aid of the state, and 236 additional miles were under contract, the total contribution of the state being about two and a half million dollars — ED

[33] Henry Clay's country seat near Lexington was called Ashland Some of his descendants still reside there.— ED.

and other such climates. By this means he has as fine grass and clover as can possibly grow. I could not but admire to see this gentleman, possessing so much knowledge and of so much weight in his country's affairs, so attentively promoting her not less important though more silent interests by improving her agriculture. What pleased me still more, however, because I less expected it, was, to hear Mrs. Clay, in priding herself on the state of society, and the rising prosperity of the country, citing as a proof the decency and affluence of the trades-people and mechanics at Lexington, many of whom ride about in their own carriages. What a contrast, both in sense and in sentiment, between this lady and the wives of Legislators (as they are called), in the land of the Boroughmongers! God grant that no privileged batch ever rise up in America, for then down come the mechanics, are harnessed themselves, and half ridden to death.

July 11*th.*—This is the hottest day we have had yet. Thermometer at 90 degrees, in shade. Met a Mr. Whittemore, from Boston, loud in the praise of this climate. He informed me he had lately lost his wife and five children near Boston, and that he should have lost his only remaining child, too, a son now stout and healthy, had he not resolved instantly to try the air of the west. He is confident that if he had taken this step in time he might have saved the lives of all his family. This might be however, and yet this climate not better than that of Boston. Spent the evening with Colonel Morrison, one of the first settlers in this state; a fine looking old gentleman, with colour in his face equal to a London Alderman.[34] The people here

---

[34] Colonel James Morrison, born in Cumberland County, Pennsylvania, was the son of an humble Irish immigrant. After serving in the Revolutionary War, he came to Kentucky, and in 1792 settled at Lexington. He

are pretty generally like that portion of the people of England who get porridge enough to eat; stout, fat, and ruddy.

July 12.— Hotter than yesterday; thermometer at 91 degrees.

July 13.— Leave Lexington; stop at Paris, 22 miles.[35] A fine country all the way; good soil, plenty of limestone and no musquitoes.   Paris is a healthy town, with a good deal of stir; woollen and cotton manufactures are carried on here, but upon a small scale.   [295] They are not near enough to good coal mines to do much in that way.   What they do, however, is well paid for.   A spinner told me he gets 83 cents per lb. for his twist, which is 33 cents more than it would fetch at New York.   Stop at Mr. Timberlake's, a good house.   The bar-keeper, who comes from England, tells me that he sailed to Canada, but he is glad he had the means to leave Canada and come to Kentucky; he has 300 dollars a year, and board and lodging.   Made enquiry after young Watson, but find he has left this place and is gone to Lexington.[36]

The following is a list of the wages and prices of the most essential branches of workmanship and articles of consumption, as they are here at present.

was successively state representative from Fayette County, president of the Lexington branch of the United States Bank, and chairman of the board of trustees of Transylvania University   Having acquired considerable wealth, he contributed liberally to educational objects, and at his death (1823) left a fund for the establishment of Morrison College, Lexington — ED.

[35] For the early history of Paris, see A Michaux's *Travels*, volume iii of our series, note 39.— ED.

[36] James Watson and his father, James Watson, senior, were both leaders of the Spenceans and by their inflammatory speeches stirred up the mob at the Spa-fields meeting (see note 6, *ante*).   The elder Watson was tried for high treason, but he was acquitted   The son escaped to America before he could be arrested — ED

	Dls	Cts		Dls	Cts
Journeymen saddlers' price for drawing on men's saddles	1	25[36]* to	—	2	50
Journeymen blacksmiths, per day	1	..	—	1	25
— Per month	25	00	— 30		
Journeymen hatters (*casters*)	1	25	—		
Ditto *rorum*	1	..	—		
Ditto for finishing, per month, and found	30		—		
Journeymen shoe-makers (*coarse*)	..	75	—		
Ditto, *fine*	1	25	—		
Ditto, for boots	3	25	—		
Journeymen tailors, by the coat	5	..	—		
Stone-masons or bricklayers, per day	1	..	—	1	50
Carpenters, per day, and found	1	..	—		
Salary for a clerk, per annum	200	..	—500		
Beef, per 100 lb.	6	..	—		
Flour, per barrel	6	..	—		

July 14th.—Hot again; 90 degrees. Arrive at Blue Licks, close by the fine Licking Creek, 22 miles from Paris.[37] Here is a sulphur and salt spring like that at French Lick in Indiana, which makes this a place of great resort in summer for the fashionable swallowers [296] of mineral waters; the three or four taverns are at this time completely crowded. Salt was made till latterly at this spring, by an old Scotsman; he now attends the ferry across the Creek. Not much to be said for the country round here; it is stony and barren, what, I have not seen before in Kentucky.

July 15th.—To Maysville, or Lime-stone, 24 miles. This is a place on the banks of the Ohio, and is a sort of port for shipping *down* the river to a great part of that

---

[36]* Or 5s. 7½d. to 11s. 3d. *sterling*. At the present rate of exchange, a *dollar* is equivalent to 4s. 6d. sterling, and a *cent* is the hundredth part of a dollar.— HULME.

[37] For the early history of Blue Licks, see Cuming's *Tour*, volume iv of our series, note 117 — ED

district of the state for which Louisville is the shipping port to and from New Orleans.[88]　Still hot; 90 degrees again.　This is the fifth day; rather unusual, this continuance of heat.　The hot spells, as well as the cold spells, seldom last more than three days, pretty generally in America.

July 16th.—Hot still, but a fine breeze blowing up the river.　Not a bit too hot for me, but the natives say it is the hottest weather they recollect in this country; a proof to me that this is a mild climate, as to heat, at any rate. Saw a cat-fish in the market, just caught out of the river by a hook and line, 4 feet long and eighty pounds weight, offered for 2 dollars.　Price of flour, 6 dollars a barrel; fresh beef, 6½ cents, and butter 20 cents per lb.

July 17th.—Set out again, crossing the Ohio into the state of that name, and take the road to Chillicothe, 74 miles from Maysville.　Stop about mid-way for the night, travelling over a country generally hilly, and not of good soil, and passing through West Union,[89] a place situated as a town ought to be, upon high and unlevel lands; the inhabitants have fine air to breathe, and plenty of food to eat and drink, and, if they keep their houses and streets and themselves clean, I will ensure them long lives. Some pretty good farms in view of the road, but many abandoned for the richer lands of Indiana and Illinois. Travelling expenses much less, hitherto, than in Indiana and some parts of Kentucky; we had plenty of good

---

[88] See A. Michaux's *Travels*, volume iii of our series, note 23, for a brief account of Maysville.— ED

[89] West Union, the seat of Adams County, is situated on Zane's Trace, seventeen miles from Maysville and fifty-five from Chillicothe.　It was established by an act of legislature (January, 1804), which fixed the county seat at that point, and ordered the land for a town to be purchased and paid for out of the county treasury.— ED.

buttermilk at the farm-houses all along the road, free of expense, and the tavern-keepers do not set before us bread made of Indian corn, which we have not yet learned to like very cordially.

[297] *July 18th.*—Come to Chillicothe,[40] the country improving and more even as we proceed. See some very rich lands on passing Paint Creek, and on approaching the Scioto river; these, like all the *bottom* lands, having a coat of sediment from their river in addition to the original soil, are by far the richest. Chillicothe is a handsome town, regularly laid out, but stands upon a flat. I hate the very sight of a level street, unless there be every thing necessary to carry off all filth and water. The air is very fine, so far as it is not contaminated by the pools of water which stand about the town as green as grass. Main sewers, like those at Philadelphia, are much wanted.

July 19th.—Called upon Mr. Bond, being introduced by letter, and spent a very pleasant evening with him and a large party of his agreeable friends.[41] Left them, much pleased with the society of Chillicothe.

July 20th.—We were introduced to Governor Worthington, who lives about 2 miles from the town.[42] He took us to his house, and showed us part of his fine estate, which is 800 acres in extent, and all of it elevated table land, commanding an immense view over the flat country in the direction of Lake Erie. The soil is very rich indeed; so

---

[40] For the early history of Chillicothe, see F. A. Michaux's *Travels*, volume iii of our series, note 35 — ED.

[41] William Key Bond was born in St. Mary's, Maryland, in 1792 Educated in Connecticut, he came to Chillicothe (1812) and was admitted to the bar. In 1841 he removed to Cincinnati, where he practiced law until his death in 1864. He was a member of the 24th, 25th, and 26th congresses, and was appointed by President Fillmore surveyor of the port of Cincinnati.— ED.

[42] For a brief biography of Governor Worthington, see Cuming's *Tour* volume iv of our series, note 142 — ED.

rich, that the governor pointed out a dung heap which was bigger than the barn it surrounded and had grown out of, as a nuisance. The labour of dragging the dung out of the way, would be more than the cost of removing the barn, so that he is actually going to pull the barn down, and build it up again in another place.   This is not a peculiarity of this particular spot of land, for manure has no value here at all.   All the stable-dung made at Chillicothe is flung into the river.   I dare say, that the Inn we put up at does not tumble into the water less than 300 good loads of horse-dung every year

I had some conversation with Governor Worthington on the subject of domestic manufactures, and was glad to find he is well convinced of the necessity of, or at least of the great benefit that would result from, the general establishment of them in the United States.   He has frequently recommended it in his public capacity, he informed me, and I hope he will [298] advocate it with effect.   He is a true lover of his country, and no man that I have met with has a more thorough knowledge of the detestable villainy of the odious Boroughmongering government of England, and, of course, it has his full share of hatred.

July 21st.— Leave Chillicothe.   A fine, healthy country and very rich land all the way to New Lancaster, 34 miles from Chillicothe, and 38 from Zanesville.[43]   Stop at the house of a German, where we slept, but not in bed, preferring a soft board and something clean for a pillow to a bed of down accompanied with bugs.

Nothing remarkable, that I can see, as to the locality of this town of *New Lancaster*; but, the name, alas! it brought to my recollection the horrid deeds done at *Old*

---

[43] For the early history of New Lancaster, see Cuming's *Tour*, volume iv of our series, note 145 — ED

Lancaster, the county town of my native country! I thought of *Colonel F——r*, and his conduct towards my poor, unfortunate townsman, Gallant! I thought of the poor, miserable creatures, men, women, and children, who, in the bloody year of 1812, were first instigated by spies to commit arson, and then pursued into death by the dealers in human blood. Amongst the sufferers upon this particular occasion, there was a boy, who was silly, and who would at any time, have jumped into a pit for a halfpenny: he was not fourteen years old; and when he was about to he hanged, actually called out for his "*mammy*" to come and save him! Who, that has a heart in his bosom, can help feeling indignation against the cruel monsters! Who can help feeling a desire to see their dreadful power destroyed! The day must come, when the whole of the bloody tragedies of Lancashire will be exposed. In the mean while, here I am in safety from the fangs of the monsters, who oppress and grind my countrymen. The thought of these oppressions, however, I carry about with me; and I cannot help its sometimes bursting forth into words.

July 22nd.— Arrived at Zanesville,⁴⁴ a place [299] finely situated for manufactures, in a nook of the Muskingham, just opposite to the mouth of Licking Creek. It has almost every advantage for manufacturing of all sorts, both as to local situation and as to materials; it excels Wheeling and Steubenville, in many respects, and, in some, even Pittsburgh. The river gives very fine falls near the town, one of them of 12 feet, where it is 600 feet wide; the creek, too, falls in by a fine cascade. What a power for machinery! I should think that as much effect

---

⁴⁴ For a more particular account of this place, as well, indeed, as of most of the other towns I have visited, see Mr Mellish's *Travels*, volume ii.— HULME.

might be produced by the power here afforded as by the
united *manual* labour of all the inhabitants of the state.
The navigation is very good all the way up to the town,
and is now continued round the falls by a canal with
locks, so that boats can go nearly close up to Lake Erie.
The bowels of the earth afford coal, iron ore, stone, free
stone, lime-stone, and *clays*: all of the best, I believe, and
the last, the very best yet discovered in this country, and,
perhaps, as good as is to be found in any country.   All
these materials are found in inexhaustible quantities in
the hills and little ridges on the sides of the river and
creek, arranged as if placed by the hand of man for his
own use.   In short, this place has the four elements in
the greatest perfection that I have any where yet seen in
America.   As to manufactures, it is, like Wheeling and
Steubenville, nothing in comparison to Pittsburg.

Nature has done her part; nothing is left wanting but
machines to enable the people of Ohio to keep their flour
at home, instead of exporting it, at their own expense to
support those abroad who are industrious enough to send
them back coats, knives, and cups, and saucers.

July 23rd.— All day at Zanesville. Spent part of it
very agreeably with Mr. Adams the post-master, and old
Mr. Dillon who has a large iron foundery near this.

July 24th.— Go with Mr. Dillon about 3 miles up the
Creek, to see his mills and iron-factory establishment. He
has here a very fine water-fall, of 18 feet, giving immense
power, by which he works a [300] large iron-forge and
foundery, and mills for sawing, grinding, and other
purposes.

I will here subjoin a list of the prices at Zanesville, of
provisions, stock, stores, labour, &c. just as I have it
from a resident, whom I can rely upon.

	Dls	Cts		Dls.	Cts.
Flour (superfine) per barrel of 196 lb. from .	5	0	to	5	75
Beef, per 100 lb.	4	0	—	4	25
Pork (prime), per 100 lb.	4	50	—	5	0
Salt, per bushel of 50 lb	2	25			
Potatoes, per bushel	0	25	—	0	31¼
Turnips, ditto	0	20			
Wheat, ditto of 60 lb. to 66 lb.	0	75			
Indian corn, ditto shelled	0	33½	—	0	50
Oats, ditto	0	25	—	0	33⅓
Rye, ditto	0	50			
Barley, ditto	0	75			
Turkeys, of from 12 lb. to 20 lb. each . .	0	37½	—	0	50
Fowls	0	12½	—	0	18¾
Live Hogs, per 100 lb. live weight . . .	3	0	—	5	0
Cows, (the best)	18	0	—	25	0
Yoke of Oxen, ditto	50	0	—	75	0
Sheep	2	50			
Hay, per ton, delivered	9	0	—	10	0
Straw, fetch it and have it.					
Manure, ditto, ditto					
Coals, per bushel, delivered	0	8			
Butter, per lb. avoirdupois	0	12½	—	0	18
Cheese, ditto, ditto	0	12½	—	0	25
Loaf Sugar	0	50			
Raw ditto	0	31¼			
Domestic Raw ditto	0	18¾			
Merino Wool, per lb. avoirdupois, washed .	1	0			
Three-quarter Merino ditto	0	75			
Common Wool	0	50			
Bricks, per 1000, delivered	6	0	—	7	0
Lime, per bushel, ditto	0	18¾			

[301] Sand, in abundance on the banks of the river.

Glass is sold in boxes, containing 100 square feet; of the common size there are 180 panes in a box, when the price is . .   14   0

The price rises in proportion to the size of the panes.

	Dls	Cts.		Dls.	Cts
Oak planks, 1 inch thick, per 100 square feet, at the saw-mill	1	50			
Poplar, the same					
White Lead, per 100 lb. delivered	17	0			
Red ditto	17	0			
Litharge	15	0			
Pig Lead	9	50			
Swedish Iron (the best, in bars)	14	0			
Juniatta, ditto, ditto	14	0			
Mr. Dillon's ditto, ditto	12	50			
Castings at Mr. Dillon's Foundery per ton	120	0			
Ditto, for machinery, ditto, per lb.	0	8			
Potash, per ton	180	0			
Pearl Ashes, ditto	200	0			
Stone masons and bricklayers, per day, and board and lodging	1	50			
Plasterers, by the square yard, they finding themselves in board and lodging and in lime, sand, laths and every thing they use.	0	18¾			
Carpenters, by the day, who find themselves and bring their tools	1	25			
Blacksmiths, by the month, found in board, lodging and tools	30	0	to	40	0
Millwrights, per day, finding themselves	1	50	—	2	0
Tailors, per week, finding themselves and working 14 or 15 hours a day	7	0	—	9	0
Shoemakers the same.					
[302] Glazier's charge for putting in each pane of glass 8 in. by 10 in. with their own putty and laying on the first coat of paint	0	4	to	0	5
Labourers, per annum; and found	100	0	—	120	0
The charge of carriage for 100 lb. weight from Baltimore to Zanisville	10	0			
Ditto for ditto by steam-boat from New Orleans to Shippingport, and thence, by boats, to Zanesville, about	6	50			
Peaches, as fine as can grow, per bushel	0	12½	—	0	25
Apples and pears proportionably cheaper; sometimes given away, in the country					

Prices are much about the same at Steubenville; if any difference, rather lower.   If bought in a quantity, some of the articles enumerated might be had a good deal lower. Labour, no doubt, if a job of some length were offered, might be got somewhat cheaper here.

July 25th — Leave Zanesville for Pittsburgh, keeping to the United States road; stop at Cambridge, 25 miles. During the first eight miles we met 10 wagons, loaded with emigrants.

July 26th. — Stop at Mr. Broadshaw's, a very good house on the road, 25 miles from Cambridge.[45]   This general government road is by no means well laid out; it goes strait over the tops of the numerous little hills, up and down, up and down.   It would have been a great deal nearer in point of time, if not in distance (though I think it would that, too), if a view had been had to the labour of travelling over these everlasting unevennesses.

July 27th. — To Wheeling in Virginia, 31 miles.   They have had tremendous rains in these parts, we hear as we pass along, lately; one of the creeks we came over has overflown so as to carry down a man's house with himself and his whole family.   A dreadful catastrophe, but, certainly, one not out of the man's [303] power to have foreseen and prevented; it surprises me that the people will stick up their houses so near the water's edge.   Cross Wheeling Creek several times to-day; it is a rapid stream, and I hope it will not be long before it turns many water-

---

[45] When in 1798 Zane's Trace was laid out from Wheeling to Zanesville, a ferry and tavern were established where the road crossed Wills Creek   Eight years later the town of Cambridge was planted.   Among the early settlers were fifteen or twenty families from the Island of Guernsey, who happened to be travelling through the West in search of homes when the town lots were offered for sale.

Bradshaw's tavern was in the village of Fairview.— Ed.

wheels. See much good land, and some pretty good farming.

July 28th.— Went with a Mr. Graham, a quaker of this place, who treated us in the most friendly and hospitable manner, to see the new national road from Washington city to this town.[46] It is covered with a very thick layer of nicely broken stones, or stone rather, laid on with great exactness both as to depth and width, and then rolled down with an iron roller, which reduces all to one solid mass. This is a road made for ever; not like the flint roads in England, rough, nor soft or dirty, like the gravel roads; but, smooth and hard. When a road *is* made in America it is *well* made. An American always plots against labour, and, in this instance, he takes the most effectual course to circumvent it. Mr. Graham took us likewise to see the fine coal mines near this place and the beds of limestone and freestone, none of which I had time to examine as we passed Wheeling in our ark. All these treasures lie very convenient to the river. The coals are principally in one long ridge, about ten feet wide; much the same as they are at Pittsburgh, in point of quality and situation. They cost 3 cents per bushel to be got out from the mine. This price, as nearly as I can calculate, enables the American collier to earn upon an average, double the number of cents for the same labour that the collier in England can earn; so that, as the American collier can, upon an average, buy his flour for one third of the price that the English collier pays for his flour, he receives *six times the quantity of flour for the same labour.* Here is a country for the ingenious paupers of England to come to! They find food and materials, and nothing want-

---

[46] For an account of the National Road, see Harris's *Journal,* volume ii of our series, note 45 — ED

ing but their mouths and hands to consume and work them. I should like to see the old toast of the Borough-mongers brought out again; when they were in the height of their impudence their myrmidons used to din in our ears, "Old England for ever, and those that do not [304] like her let them leave her." Let them renew this swaggering toast, and I would very willingly for my part, give another to the same effect for the United States of America. But, no, no! they know better now. They know that they would be taken at their word; and, like the tyrants of Egypt, having got their slaves fast, will (if they can) keep them so. Let them beware, lest something worse than the Red Sea overwhelm them. Like Pharaoh and his Boroughmongers they will not yield to the voice of the people, and, surely, something like, or worse than, their fate shall befall them!

They are building a steam-boat at Wheeling, which is to go, they say, 1800 miles up the Missouri river. The wheels are made to work in the stern of the boat, so as not to come in contact with the floating trees, snaggs, planters,[47] &c., obstructions most likely very numerous in that river. But, the placing the wheels behind only saves *them*; it is no protection against the *boat's sinking* in case of being pierced by a planter or sawyer.[48] Observing this I will suggest a plan which has occurred to me, and which, I think, would provide against sinking, effectually; but, at any rate, it is one which can be tried very easily and with very little expense.— I would make a partition of strong plank; put it in the broadest fore-part of the boat, right across, and put good iron bolts under the bottom of the boat, through these planks, and screw them on

---

[47] Trees tumbled head-long and fixed in the river — HULME.

[48] The same as the planter only waving up and down — HULME

the top of the deck. Then put an upright post in the in-
side of the boat against the middle of the plank partition,
and put a spur to the upright post. The partition should
be water-tight. I would then load the fore-part of the
boat, thus partitioned off with lumber or such loading as
is least liable to injury, and best calculated to stop the
progress of a sawyer after it has gone through the boat
— By thus appropriating the fore-part of the boat to the
reception of planters and sawyers, it appears to me that
the other part would be secured against all·intrusion.

[305] *July 29th.*— From Wheeling, through Charlston, changing sides of the river again to Steubenville.⁴⁰
My eyes were delighted at Charlston to see the smoke of
the coals ascending from the glass-works they have here.
This smoke it is that must enrich America; she might
save almost all her dollars if she would but bring her in-
valuable black diamonds into service. Talk of inde-
pendance, indeed, without coats to wear or knives or
plates to eat with!

At Steubenville, became acquainted with Messrs. Wills,
Ross, and company, who have an excellent and well-con-
ducted woollen manufactory here. They make very good
cloths, and at reasonable prices; I am sorry they do not
retail them at Philadelphia; I for one, should be customer
to them for all that my family wanted in the woollen-
way. Here are likewise a Cotton-mill, a Grist-mill, a
Paper-mill, an Iron-foundery and Tan-yards and Brew-

⁴⁰ Charleston, on the Kanawha River, about sixty miles from its mouth, is
located on the military grant made by Lord Dunmore to Colonel Thomas
Bullitt (1772), in recognition of his services in Braddock's and Forbes's cam-
paigns. Five years thereafter, the land was purchased by George Clendenin,
one of the commissioners for laying out a road from Lewisburg to the Kanawha
Clendenin constructed (1788) a fort on the present site of Charleston, and soon
other pioneers built log cabins under its shelter. In 1794 the town of Charleston was established by legislative enactment.— ED

eries.   Had the pleasure to see Mr. Wilson,[60] the editor
of the Steubenville Gazette, a very public-spirited man,
and, I believe, very serviceable to this part of the country.   If the policy he so powerfully advocates were
adopted, the effects would be grand for America; it
would save her dollars while it would help to draw the
nails of the vile Boroughmongers.   But, he has to labour
against the inveterate effects of the thing the most diffi-
cult of all others to move — habit.

By what I have been able to observe of this part of the
country, those who expect to find what is generally understood by *society*, pretty much the same that they have
been accustomed to it on the Atlantic side, or in England,
will not be totally disappointed.   It is here upon the basis
of the same manners and customs as in the oldest settled
districts, and it there differs from what it is in England,
and here from what it is there, only according to circum-
stances.   Few of the social amusements that are practicable at present, are scarce; dancing, the most rational
for every reason, is the most common; and in an assemblage for this purpose, composed of the farmers' daughters and sons from 20 miles round, an Englishman (par-
ticularly if a young one) might very well think his travels
to be [306] all a dream, and that he was still in a Borough-
monger country.   Almost always the same tunes and
dances, same manners, same dress.   Ah, it is that same
dress which is the great evil!   It may be a very pretty
sight, but, to see the dollars thus danced out of the country into the hands of the Boroughmongers, to the tune

---

[60] James Wilson, who had been on the staff of the Philadelphia *Aurora*,
came to Steubenville (1815) to edit the *Herald*, changing the name to the *Western Herald and Steubenville Gazette*, and the politics from Democratic to Whig.
Wilson was elected to the state legislature in 1816 and again in 1820, and was
an associate justice of the court of common pleas   He died in 1852.— ED.

of national airs, is a thing which, if it do not warrant ridicule, will, if America do not, by one unanimous voice, soon put a stop to it.

July 30th.— From Steubenville, crossing the Ohio for the last time, and travelling through a slip of Virginia and a handsome part of Pennsylvania, to Pittsburgh.

August 1st.— Sold my horse for 75 dollars, 60 dollars less than I gave for him. A horse changes masters no where so often as in this Western country, and no where so often rises and falls in value. Met a Mr. Gibbs, a native of Scotland, and an old neighbour of mine, having superintended some oil of vitriol works, near to my bleach-works on Great Lever, near Bolton, in Lancashire. He now makes oil of vitriol, aquafortis, salt, soap, &c. at this place, and is, I believe, getting rich. Spent a pleasant evening with him.

August 2nd.— Spent most part of the day with Mr. Gibbs, and dined with him; as the feast was his, I recommended him to observe the latter part of the good Quaker Lady's sermon which we heard at New Albany.

August 3rd.— Leave Pittsburgh, not without some regret at bidding adieu to so much activity and smoke, for I expect not to see it elsewhere. I like to contemplate the operation by which the greatest effect is produced in a country. Take the same route and the same stage as on setting out from Philadelphia.

August 4th, 5th, and 6th.— These three days traversing the romantic Allegany Mountains; got overturned (a common accident here) *only* once, and then received very little damage: myself none, some of my fellow travellers a few scratches. We scrambled out, and, with the help of some wagoners, set the vehicle on its wheels again, adjusted our ''*plunder*'' (as some of the Western people call it), and drove on again [307] without being detained more than five minutes. The fourth night slept at Chambersburgh, the beginning of a fine country.

August 7th.— Travelled over the fine lime-stone valley before mentioned, and through a very good country all the way, by Little York to Lancaster. Here I met with a person from Philadelphia, who told me a long story about a *Mr. Hulme*, an Englishman, who had brought a large family and considerable property to America. His property, he told me, the said Mr. Hulme had got from the English Government, for the invention of some machine, and that now, having got rich under their patronage, he was going about this country doing the said Government all the mischief he could, and endeavouring to promote the interest of this country. After letting him go on till I was quite satisfied that he depends mainly for his bread and butter upon the English Treasury, I said, ''Well, do you know this Mr. Hulme?'' ''No, he had only heard of him.'' ''Then I do, and I know that he never had any patent, nor ever asked for one, from the English government; all he has got he has gained by his own industry and economy, and, so far from receiving a fortune from that vile government, he had nothing to do with it but to pay and obey, without being allowed to give a vote for a Member of Parliament or for any Government officer. He is now, thank God, in a country where he cannot be taxed but by his own consent, and, if he should succeed in contributing in any degree to the downfall of the English Government, and to the improvement of this country, he will only succeed in doing his duty.'' This man could be no other than a dependant of that boroughmongering system which has its feelers probing every quarter and corner of the earth.

August 8th.— Return to Philadelphia, after a journey of 72 days. My expenses for this journey, including every thing, not excepting the loss sustained by the purchase and sale of my horse, amount to 270 dollars and 70 cents.

As it is now about a twelvemonth since I have [308] been settled in Philadelphia, or set foot in it, rather, with my family, I will take a look at my books, and add to this Journal what have been the expenses of my family for this one year, from the time of landing to this day, inclusive.

		Dls.	Cts.
House-rent		600	0
Fuel		137	'0
Schooling (at day-schools) for my children viz.; Dolls			
for Thomas, 14 years of age 40			
Peter and John, ages of 12 and 10 48			
Sarah, 6 years of age . . . . 18 —		106	0
Boarding of all my family at Mrs. Anthony's Hotel			
for about a week, on our arrival		80	0
Expenses of house-keeping (my family fourteen in			
number, including two servants) with every other			
out-going not enumerated above, travelling inci-			
dents, two newspapers a day, &c., &c.		2076	66
Taxes, not a cent		0	0
Priest, not a cent		0	0

Total 2999 66

"What! nothing to the Parson!" some of my old neighbours will exclaim. No: not a single stiver. The Quakers manage their affairs without Parsons, and I believe they are as good and as happy a people as any religious denomination who are aided and assisted by a Priest. I do not suppose that the Quakers will admit me into their Society; but, in this free country I can form a new society, if I choose, and, if I do, it certainly shall be a Society having a Chairman in place of a Parson, and the assemblage shall discuss the subject of their meeting themselves. Why should there not be as much knowledge and wisdom and common sense, in the heads of a whole congregation, as in the head of a Parson? Ah, but then there are the profits arising from the trade! Some of this holy Order in England receive upwards of 40,000 dollars per [309] annum for preaching probably not more than five or six sermons during the whole year. Well may the Cossack Priests represent Old England as the bulwark of religion! This is the sort of religion they so much dreaded the loss of during the French Revolution; and this is the sort of religion they so zealously expected to establish in America, when they received the glad tidings of the restoration of the Bourbons and the Pope.

END OF THE JOURNAL